PARADE

www.ingramcontent.com/pod-product-compliance
Lightning Source LLC
LaVergne TN
LVHW051217070526
838200LV00063B/4944

OF

PAST

LIVES

K.A. RAMIL

First published in August 2024 by
Poetry Global Network
Unit A
82 James Carter Road
Mildenhall
Suffolk, England
IP28 7DE

@thepgnofficial
www.poetryglobalnetwork.com

ISBN: 978-1-7392881-9-8

Copyright (c) Poetry Global Network, Ltd (UK), 2024

The rights of the named poets to be identified as the author of their work is in accordance with the Copyright, Designs and Patents Act 1998.

Editors: Mark Fishbein, Phynne~Belle
Cover photo by David Reyna (DRMadeIt.com)

All rights reserved. No part of this book may be reproduced, stored or transmitted in any form or by any means (electronic or mechanical) without prior written permission of the publisher and the author.

Parade of Past Lives

K.A. RAMIL

CONTENTS

Becoming
5

An Act of Imitation
9

my name spelled in doubts
10

The Body: A Continent
11

at the river's mouth
12

stillness
13

Conversations
17

Absence
19

Dear Other
20

Coming Home
21

In Between: Crossroads
22

In Between: Horizons
23

In Between: Transits
24

Reflex
25

Tequila Sunrise
26

The Day After
31

Among the Crowd
32

from my room
33

Because the City Was Empty
34

Time's Up
35

To be Seen
36

The Thereafter
37

ACKNOWLEDGEMENTS

Some poems have previously appeared in the following journals:

>*Conversations* (The Hong Kong Review)
>*Coming Home* (Full House Literary)
>*Tequila Sunrise* (Santa Clara Review)

My deepest gratitude—

To DC Collective—Mark, Elizabeth, Prosser, Jay, Steve, **Shulamit, and most especially, David Siller**—for helping fashion most of the pieces in this collection into their final forms.

To Maya Popa for taking the time to strengthen *stillness* into the piece that it is.

To all the people who took me as a passenger and made the journey worth writing.

To *Lakay Ipe* and *Baket Goling*.

*For the wanderers.
Never cease to wonder.*

Becoming

To choose myself, despite myself,
I learned where to stand—

Roots don't care, they thrive in the dark.
Wind won't win against the sound

rolling on the street—wheels
& blisters. After chasing enough twisters,

I became a hurricane. The air too much,
the lungs can no longer accommodate the heart.

There are names I swallowed frozen
in the cords. My voice tasted rust,

an acquired sound the way trees lean
to defy breaking.

I learned where to stand—
To choose myself despite myself.

An Act of Imitation

I'm a work in progress, says a bodybuilder. So am I. For five days, I cut sequence shots into a montage. For five minutes a day, I act like a residual version of Bond, James Bond. In those five minutes, I *man up*. Hollywood in my mind. When the movie stops, I am just another towel soaked in warm water—soothing sore muscles. Still, I am becoming. Unlike Michaelanglo's *Atlas*—trapped in the *non finito* marble blocks. I will take my time in the box even as a jack.

my name
spelled in doubts

il mio nome non sai! Turandot, Act III

call me anything—anyone's name—but mine.
already heard it in a hundred different rhymes—letters

play, trading places. my room floor slopes
where it should be even. the ink bleeds off the pages

forging the fear of falling into gospel. nothing
is permanent enough. i cannot stay in my room

or just stay—*here*—at all. a bookmark
between chapters, dried flat flowers. again,

call me what you want as i try to get a sense of *i*.
say it—*louder, please*—until it lends clarity,

until the echoes become the voice, the flood
into blood, until i'm certain a rendezvous remains

where i tell my own tales.

The Body: A Continent

My fingertips are suddenly alien to touch.
I search for the fractures,
there's a new one each count.

Maybe I gave   too much too fast—

the floating bone under my smaller lung
& for once, I want to slow down.

Inhale

Exhale

Strum the cage, rearrange my ribs—

an attempt at rhythm

        to claim

what remains
        of myself

of my body

even as its plates have shifted & coalesced

one by one

        —a pangaea in memoriam.

at the river's mouth

we always talk about the river,
how mighty it was.
how it forged its shape
in the pastoral. how it understood
the depth of silence, the anguish
of those who wept on its bank.
how it's stepped into only once.

we always talk about the river,
seldom about the boulders that chipped themselves
into trenches, the sediments that settled,
the sand that rolled into pebbles.

to hold the current steady, topography gave way.

so let me spend a lifetime—
what's left of it—to race the rapids,
feel the centuries under my feet,
& discover stones that hold hopes
in its mouth.

stillness

i may never master the sleight of hand
though i know its science,
its physics of trajectory & velocity.
stubborn is the body, its muscle
memory. you—taught me skipping stones,
pebbles at my windows,
curtains drawn shut. you who woke up
earlier than hunger.
who said *let's go!*
but then went ahead,
far ahead—
      a stone launched at 20°, the magic angle, then spun
in a straight line, the shortest line—
            away from me.
abruptly.
    to *enjoy—just enjoy!*
is a lesson i needed to learn, you said.
you always said.

i've learned to hold the hour hand in the same riverside
where i witnessed more going than coming.
stood in silence
      for too long i will never
      be a stone.

Conversations

I

Words whispered—
most meant, some escaped
without warning. Always
too late.

Silence followed—
the kind that calls my name
in its profound quietude. I'm learning
to trust my body
again. My ears ring,
senses flood at times when I prefer to rather
not feel

       anything.

ii

Over mojos and pizza on a partly cloudy night, I waited for your usual version of the day's whatabouts: the return demos, the surgery gloves—hands up, palms selfward. *I'm tired.* Sometimes, leaves fall without turning color. I caught *What if I don't care* in the Radio City elevator ride. I dropped *Let's end it here* during a morning jog on 11th Ave, when a forest was too far around. There were 470,000 entries in the unabridged Webster's Third New International Dictionary. The second edition of the Oxford version reported the same number. Yet for weeks, I reached for words—to cross, to walk upon, to tiptoe on. You said *New York is waving!* one early morning in early spring but instead of crossing the bridge, I was flooded by the depth of the water running under it.

iii

Words
                Silence

Words in between silence
Silence in between words

A perpetual search for a victor when I—
All I want is to punch the mirror.

Absence

There are no shadows in cocoons—
only clouds in an endless slope of darkness
waiting for its ultimate shape.
Keep hanging.
Don't fall on the floor stripped of carpet.
In the long winter slumber
when grass was eager to spring,
I tried to call your name.
Perhaps it didn't catch you.
Perhaps my voice was an owl
flying, slow in its silence.
In contrast to our long motorcycle rides
at almost 100 kms/hr.
Almost.
Hands on the handlebar,
my shoulders quite tight.

Relax

To exist beside you & not with you:
I am gone because I
wanted to go.

Dear Other

The kettle starts to whistle. I wake up
to an allergy, to blessed sneezes, but I won't skip
any chance to sleep.
The bus departs at 6:00—that I'd rather miss.
My favorite route takes Vivaldi's all seasons
to reach the destination.
To truly live, leave things then watch them vanish.
Your turn.
Too early for promises so heavy.
Let me exist in the lyrics I envy—
your hands. An experience. I tell the world
pieces that it will remember
when I'm tired of trying.

I was always trying.

      I am trying.

Your coffee mug still sits unwashed in the sink.

Coming Home

The red luggage awaits unpacking.
Remnants—I wonder
how many bodies have I shifted into.
No, I don't hate this body nor the skins I've shed—
given choice, given time
again I will leave.
Unlike my friends, the friends who grew
faster than everyone,
my mannequin accumulated dust
in someone else's warehouse.
There were wishes written on my father's bones,
stories of comfort & vision.

Time to open that he'd say

& watch me

        take out   each   shirt.

Tell me, is that his scent?

In Between: Crossroads

It's 5:55 on the clock as I pass by
my favorite burger stand—closed: WE'VE MOVED!

The chalk bleeding, the red light's stalling.

Synchronicities appear
when I stop looking, sudden prodding
when I slow down breathing—
deeper, fuller—filling the empty
crevices
I never knew existed.

I spent years from the passenger side—
rolled the windows up & down,
blasted the stereo, rewound cassettes.
I have seen a lot & still not enough.
Before slowing down,
blood circulates at 3 ft/sec as it leaves the heart.
My veins rolled out of my hands gasping for light.

It's easy to blame the traffic for being stuck
at intersections, addresses I changed at an impulse.

I remember each one:

> The painted walls, shades of sunsets—
> clouds hanging, bridges burning.

As the traffic light turns yellow.

In Between: Horizons

I learned to draw early, traced full circles
instead of short straight lines for beginners.

I made life into a bubble out of embraces
until it bruised into bursts of small & smaller circles.

I invited the sun so close my pulse ruptured
into solar flares. Made a tunnel out of light.

I walked through it. Or around.
It only mattered that I'm walking forward.

If I squint hard enough, sometimes I see a whirlpool.
Sometimes I feel like walking back.

But I'm not the vanishing point.
In a still photograph, I'm the persistent motion.

I've drawn fences into boundaries,
to not live in the illusion of space.

In Between: Transits

Limes sliced, tequila uncapped.
But first I said & set the Review on your lap.
You read my poem, running your fingers
on every letter—became pensive, then asked

Did it come back?

I pushed the shot glass—
Too caught up to answer.
Too caught up to lie.
You closed the book. On the cover, a person
reaching out—like me—forward & outward.
But I've learned where to search,
watch myself. Still pose questions, got bolder
declarations. The unfinished
bottle stands on the countertop,
the salt shaker on its side.
   Dust—gathering around.
We couldn't stay. In suitcases,
mastered to fit in years, waited at gates.
There'll be onboardings. In abundance

of words, what I say remains

        only half the answer.

Reflex

I wanted to learn
the dynamics of forgetting
the way babies develop the reflex
to grasp at an object.
How it disappears in about six months.
A perfect disappearing act.
Perfect for dropping the weight of selfish memories:
Bicycle rides home under the rising sun.
Time-stamped polaroids
when everyone was lost in trance.
There's drowning, then there's drought.
I wanted to live out of the water, outside that box.
Matches too damp to ignite.

Say *bukas* and mean open. Or mean tomorrow.

Yesterday was too far.

    I am here—now.

        A reminder, an open memory.

And we remember things very differently.

Tequila Sunrise

It called for a celebration—
       or mourning, depending
on where you stand
       under the collapsing
light of the streetlamp.

The daybreak came sudden and to say
it was a surprise—
       a lie, a make-believe that the night
will last despite the omens at dusk:

       the presence of murders
of crows in flyover,
       the absence of notes
                    sparrows make
when perched on the wires of the posts
      along the road creating a secret sonata

& so secretly, I expected not
my white dove to come back,

      with a stalk of rice
      or an olive branch.

     You   burned my wings
    I   collected the ashes

    Is that completion enough in itself?

The cycle proceeds & I refused to stop—
resolved to control only those at grasp:

    the fire in the glass,
    the sunrise in the shots.

The Day After

Tell me again about the night you chased the year
      & life pulled you over.
      How you introduced yourself, each syllable
an air of knowing.
      How recognition dawned like concrete
curing on its own. Your ancestors
      were farmers, their ancestors gatherers.
  They left you
with hunger, an appetite you mistook for longing.

Look at all the invitations: the living & then the leaving.

So much time spent deciding.

      That means doubt. That means you've waited long enough.

That means you can abandon all the things you've known.

Before that night.

Among
the Crowd

According to Feng Shui, in a room,
stay in command position

to see everything forthcoming.

Be it chaos or silence
& never in between.

Be able to whisper, make its loudness
distinct. A door shut tight

swung open, let myself in.

Parties. Balconies. Jack Daniel's.
Small talks. Tiptoes

down a rabbit hole. Holed

up & let hold. I stood on the platform,
watched the train leave the station.

Thoughts. Desires. Fire—

extinguished but remained
highly susceptible to ignition.

Forward. Toward. Cast

afterthoughts into plans. No more
waiting for replies.

from my room

i still see the pond, what it used to be.
i remember the gravel path towards it,
stones crushing, adjusting under my weight.

wind gust into the door
so heavy it remains a door. see, all doors
are the same—a welcome to some balance
like stones stacked steady. then enters entropy,
at first gradually

then all at once.

the pond dried up, the downslope
leveled, bricks mortared into a house,
into translucent walls of glass.

maybe i'm a wall

& have always been—a wall eavesdropping on a secret.

let me be home to hold it.

Because the City Was Empty

I left—I ran away
from the rain only to catch more of it.

Anywhere else is better
until the laughters on the streets
cobbled with memories faded
into an echo, into a faint, familiar rousing

    —go!

Then like a kite snapped into flight, welcomed the wind
into a parade of all my past lives. I could not

become who I already was.

    I forgot the string.

    I forgot there is a string.

Like how water expands as it evaporates,
its volume increases, becomes less dense.

So maybe it's this: the city was empty because I left.

Time's Up

In a game of hide-and-seek, there is so much
to find:
Behind me a forest;
no solace, only imminence.

And in this game of hide-and-seek, I'm tired
of hiding—

>*Ready or not here I come.*

>All those people I found
>couldn't be a win if I end up

>to myself, a stranger.

To
Be Seen

Show me how you dialed the camera
& slowed down time. How every turn made us younger.

How we used our youth as currency
to visit every city where our fingers fell off.

How we gathered, reassembled them
in an attempt at wholeness.

Let there be wholeness.

Forget the fractions fractured by hanging on the ledge,
on its very edge thinking there wasn't enough space.

There wasn't enough—

So we bargained too much. We couldn't afford
sincerity even at its most discounted.

We searched for the reflections we kissed
goodbye & found smudges no one dared to wipe.

We let the light in, refracted it to the ceiling of the room
that held our bones to set. We watched it
the way light was in awe the first time it saw a rainbow
only to learn it is *itself*
        in various waves.

Even light has parts waiting to be named.

The Thereafter

I laughed until

I cried when they opened my body
& my heart leapt into another time.

It rearranged the universe at will with its memory in slivers:
an unreturned call, a frameless mirror, an untitled nocturne—

a body
without a name;
a name
without a body.

A feedback loop in short circuit.
A whole life reduced to eulogies.

There goes a promise of everything, the entitlement to the world.
But shoes were paired at the doorstep, height measured in hours.

There were frontiers to conquer,
ceilings to shatter, lines to cross.

In the end there's a thump, nothing follows.

Only a thump,

a thump

then silence—

About the Author

K.A. Ramil is an accountant by license and a storyteller by passion. He lives in a small town in the northeast of the Philippines. His works have appeared in *The Hong Kong Review, Santa Clara Review, Full House Literary*, and others.